A fun Guide just ♥ for Girls ages 6-9

Just For Me!
Friends

Katrina Cassel

LEGACY PRESS®

Dedication:

To Jasmine and Ariana, second generation friends.

A special thanks to:

The Legacy team for all the creativity they add to their books;
Jessica for reading through the first draft and checking the
puzzles; Tyler for his computer help; Teresa for always being
there when I need suggestions; and Rick for being my best
friend for life.

JUST FOR ME: FRIENDS
©2007 by Legacy Press
ISBN 10: 1-58411-082-1
ISBN 13: 978-1-58411-082-8
Legacy reorder#: LP48411
JUVENILE NONFICTION / Religion / Christianity / Christian Life

Legacy Press
P.O. Box 261129
San Diego, CA 92196

Cover and Interior Illustrator: Dave Carlson

Scriptures are from the *Holy Bible: New International Version* (North
American Edition), ©1973, 1978, 1984 by the International Bible
Society. Used by permission of Zondervan Bible Publishers.

Printed in the United States of America

Table of Contents

Hi Girlfriend!

Good friends are such an important part of our lives. **Learning to make and keep friends** is a skill that you will use your whole life. This book will help you:

✳ Learn some great things that friends do for each other

✳ Find out the best character traits to look for in friends -- and in yourself

✳ Discover places to make new friends

✳ Learn how to make new friends

✳ Discover more about your best friend

✳ Solve friendship problems

✳ Find lots of fun games and activities to do with friends — or by yourself

✳ Learn more about your very best friend ever

In *Just for Me: Friends*, **you'll find advice and suggestions about friendships,** and you'll also find fun puzzles, Bible verses, and stories about friends.

4

There are crafts, games, questions and prayers for you to enjoy. So get involved and try out all the fun stuff inside! Most of all you'll have fun finding and making friends. And you'll learn about your best friend of all – Jesus!

What is a Friend?

Chapter 1

Friends come in all shapes and sizes. Friends may be younger or older than you are. **Bigger or smaller.** They may be the same color as you or different. Your friends might be from school, a home school group or from church. They might live in your neighborhood or farther away.

Girls' Stories **Three sets of Friends**

Brianna, Leah and Kathryn all play on the same softball team. They have fun practicing together. Sometimes their moms drive them to the city pool so they can swim together too.

Courtney and David have always lived next door to each other. There are no other girls in their neighborhood so Courtney always plays with David. They ride their bikes around the block or play games in Courtney's house.

Emily, Hannah and Madison all go to Jefferson Elementary School. They live only a few blocks from the school so they walk to school together. Sometimes they leave for school early so that they have time to play on the playground together.

What do you think of when someone says "friend"? Do you think of someone like the kids in the stories above? Do you think of someone who:

*listens to your problems?

*cares when you are sad?

*cheers you on when you're up to bat?

*helps you with a hard math problem?

*plays with you at recess?

*laughs with you when you're happy?

Friends are really important, aren't they? Can

you imagine how boring life would be without friends? Who would you eat lunch with at school? Who would you walk with to school? Who would come to your birthday party or invite you to hers? Friends are a

valuable part of our everyday lives! The most important part of friends is who they are on the inside.

True Friends

Think about words that describe your friends. Try to think of one description for each letter in the word "friend." You might use words that tell

about your friend's
personality. You
might write down
activities that your
friend and you like to
do together. You can
even write down your
favorite foods.

Here's an example:

NoW YOU Try!

F - funny

F -

R - runs fast

R -

i - ice cream

i -

E - excited

E -

N - nice

N -

D - draws well

D -

These words help answer the question:

"What is a friend?"

Puzzle Pieces

Have you ever done a picture puzzle? Each piece is different. Each one adds something new to the puzzle. You and your friends are like that. Each of you is different, but each of you adds something to the

friendship. Some of your friends might be tall. Others are short. Some may be good at math while others are better at reading. You might have friends who like sports and friends who like to read or draw. God made you in a special way. He made each friend in a special way, too.

Bible Wisdom

Psalm 139 talks about how God Made You & Your Friends. Verse 14 says, *"I praise you because I am ...wonderfully made."*

✳ Praying

Write a prayer to God and thank Him for making you special.

Dear God,

_____

_____

_____

Love,_____

 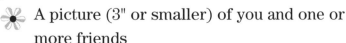

❖ Friendship Frame ❖

You can make an easy frame to hold a picture of yourself and a friend. The picture will remind you that you are special to God.

▶ You Will Need

✳ A picture (3" or smaller) of you and one or more friends

✳ Four craft sticks

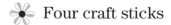

Small puzzle pieces from a spare puzzle (ask for permission!)

Paint, buttons, sequins, stickers or other small items to decorate your frame. Choose items that show your personality.

Tape

String or yarn

 ## What to do

Arrange the craft sticks around the edge of your picture to see how big to make your frame.

Remove the picture and glue the sticks together to form a frame. It's okay if the sticks overlap or you have extra hanging over the end.

Paint the puzzle pieces. You can make them all one color or many colors. Allow the paint to dry.

Glue puzzle pieces on the frame. The frame will look better if you do one layer of pieces side-by-side and then put another layer overlapping those. Allow the glue to dry.

- Glue decorations on the puzzle pieces. Allow the glue to dry.

- Put a strip of glue around the edge of your picture. Place the frame over the picture. Allow the glue to dry.

- Tape string to the top of the back of the picture for hanging the picture.

That's What Friends Are For

Chapter 2

Having friends is fun, isn't it? You can play games, ride your bikes, make crafts, talk, draw and a whole lot more together. You can also talk about problems and share secrets together. It doesn't matter if you have one or two close friends or a whole bunch — life is just better with buddies to share it. Why? Read on and you'll find out!

There are three important things that friends do for each other:

*Friends listen to each other
*Friends care when you are sad
*Friends keep secrets

Step by Step Friends Listen To Each Other

Do you have fun talking with your friends? You might talk about school. You might share what happened when your grandmother visited. Or you might tell about what your brother did at dinner last night. You may want to tell your friend about something funny that your dog did. Maybe you want to talk about an activity that you want to try. Friends are good listeners no matter what.

 ## Is That a Horse or a Dog?

Alexis ran out of the school building and looked for her friend Samantha. They walked home from school together every day.

"Wasn't art class the best today?" Alexis asked.

"Yes! I learned a lot about drawing," Samantha said.

"Me too," Alexis said. "But my drawing of a horse looked more like a dog!"

✴ **Just for Me!** ✴

"My picture looked kind of funny, too," Samantha said. "But I still had fun. I hope we work on drawing again next week!"

 ## What do You Talk about with Friends?

Alexis and Samantha like to walk home together and talk about their day at school. What is something that you can talk to a friend about? Pretend that the pictures below are you and a friend talking. Write what you would say in your word bubble. Write what your friend might say in the other bubble.

Color the girls to look like you and your friend.

Bible Wisdom

It's fun to talk with your friends. The way that you talk with your friends makes a difference. The book of Proverbs tells us something about the words we say to others. To find out what it says, look at the letter under each line. Write the letter that comes next in the alphabet on the line (A comes after Z). The first one is done to help you.

P _ _ _ _ _ _ _   _ _ _ _ _
o   k   d   z   r   z   m   s   v   n   q   c   r

_ _ _ ... _ _ _ _ _   _ _
z   q   d   r   v   d   d   s   s   n

_ _ _   _ _ _ _.
s   g   d   r   n   t   k

—Proverbs 16:24

That verse from Proverbs is true, isn't it? Your words can be sweet just like chocolate.

21

✳Step byStep✳ Friends Care When You Are Sad

In Romans 12:15, the Bible tells us what we should do when others are happy or sad. It says to be happy with those who are happy and sad with those who are sad.

These pictures show a friend being happy with another friend and a friend caring about a sad friend. Decorate these two pictures with your favorite colors.

 # What Would You Do?

Read the sentences below. They tell about situations that could happen at your school. Read each one and write down what you would do.

1. You notice that a girl in your class is sitting at the end of the lunch table by herself. She looks upset, and she's not eating her lunch. What would you do?

_____

_____

2. You get invited to a birthday party, but your friend doesn't get an invitation. She's very disappointed. What would you do?

_____

_____

3. You did great on your math test. Your friend got a lot of problems wrong. You can tell that she's really upset. What would you do?

_____

_____

There is no one right answer for these questions, Here are some possible answers that build friendships:

▶ For number one, you could sit by the girl or ask her to join you and your friends. You might talk to her and find out why she seems upset and isn't eating.

▶ For number two, perhaps you could tell your friend you were sorry she didn't get an invitation and offer to spend some extra time with her another day.

For number three, you might offer to help her with her math homework. You could help her study for the next math test.

 **Friends Keep Secrets**

Another special part of friendship is telling each other secrets. You do that because you feel close to each other. Sharing secrets is fun, isn't it?

Girls' Stories   Talk to Me!

"Can I tell you a secret?" Latisha asked her friend Melissa.

"Of course," Melissa said.

"My mom is going to have a baby. She doesn't want everyone to know yet," Latisha said, "but I need someone I can talk to about it. I wonder how having a new baby will change things. I wonder if my mom will still have time for me."

"I won't tell anyone about the new baby until you say I can," Melissa said. "And you can talk to me about it any time."

"Thanks," Latisha said. "You are a good friend. I know I can trust you to keep my secret."

Latisha told Melissa her secret because they were good friends. Latisha knew she could trust Melissa not to tell anyone else. Do you have friends you can share your secrets with and know they won't tell anyone else? Write their names here:

_____

_____

_____

Bible Wisdom

Did you know that the book of Proverbs in the Bible talks about what kind of person keeps a secret?

Put the words below in order on the train cars so that you can read the verse. One word is filled in to help you.

trustworthy a A
secret keeps

man

—Proverbs 11:13

This verse says "man", but it is true for anyone. This verse means that a person who can be trusted keeps a secret. The only time you should tell a secret is if a friend tells you she is being hurt by someone or if she is going to do something that will hurt herself or others.

 Can you think of a **fun secret to share** with your friends today?

_____

_____

Share the secret with the friends whose names you wrote on page 26. Write down what each friend says when you tell her the secret.

_____

_____

Friends listen when you talk, friends care when you're sad, and friends keep secrets. **But that's not all** friends do for each other!

Being a Good Friend

Chapter 3

Step byStep Friends Like You for Who You Are

Do all of your friends look alike? Do they all act the same? Of course not! Some friends are tall and others are short. Some have blonde hair and others have black hair. Some have freckles and others have glasses. Friends might be quiet or noisy, silly or serious. Friends like each other for who they are even when they are different.

You're Too Short!

Destiny and Kayla stood in line for the roller coaster at the fair.

"I don't think I'm tall enough for this ride," Kayla said.

"I don't have to worry about that!" Destiny said with a laugh.

Kayla is the shortest girl in third grade and Destiny is the tallest. That isn't the only difference between them. Kayla has red hair and freckles. Destiny has black hair and brown skin. Kayla likes craft projects with beads and braiding. Destiny likes sports better.

"You're too short," the man running the ride told Kayla.

"I'll skip this ride, too," Destiny said.

"No, you go ahead. I'll wait for you right here," Kayla said.

"Okay. You get to pick the next ride," Destiny said.

Kayla waited while Destiny went on the ride. "I don't think I would have liked that ride anyway," she told her when Destiny got off of it.

"It was awesome," Destiny said. "But we don't have to like the same rides. We're different in lots of ways, but you're my best friend anyway."

Step by Step We're All Different

It's good to have a lot of different kinds of friends. Each friend has something unique about her that makes your friendship special. God planned it that way. He made each person in a unique and special way. It would be boring if everyone looked and acted the same way as each other. God wants you

to accept your friends for who He made them to be.

 ## YOU said it! Friendly Faces

Some of your friends may be tall and others short. They may have different colored hair or skin. Draw your friends on the following pages. Or, if you have pictures of your friends, glue them over the face. Then fill in the blanks about your friends.

Friend's Name:

_____

_____

Best thing about him/her:

_____

_____

_____

_____

Activities We Both Like:

_____

_____

_____

_____

_____

_____

_____

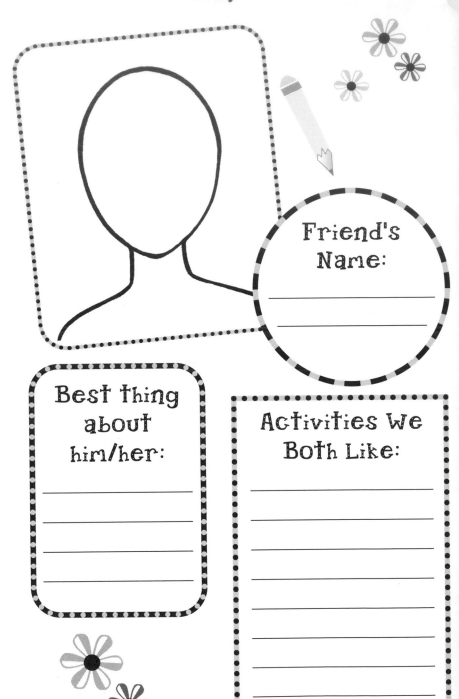

Friend's Name:

_____

_____

Best thing
about
him/her:

_____

_____

_____

_____

Activities We
Both Like:

_____

_____

_____

_____

_____

_____

_____

_____

Write a letter to God and thank Him for the special differences between you and your friends.

Dear God,

_____

_____

_____

_____

Your child,

_____

Bible Wisdom

It's important that you accept your friends the way that God made them. What does God say about accepting each other? Cross out every "w" in the verse below. Write the rest of the letters in order on the lines and you will be able to read the message.

A W C C E W P T   W O W N E   W A N O T H W E R

__ __ __ __ __   __ __ __   __ __ __ __ __ __ __

... J W U S T   W A S   C W H R I W S T

__ __ __ __   __ __   __ __ __ __ __ __

W A C C W E P T E D   W Y O U.

__ __ __ __ __ __ __   __ __ __.

— Romans 15:7

✳Step byStep✳ Friends Spend Time Together

It's fun to spend time with friends. You can play or talk, draw or ride bikes, jump rope or shoot baskets. A friend can teach you a new activity. You can teach your friend something that you know how to do. You might do different activities with different friends.

Danielle and Morgan were playing on the swings at the park. A girl they didn't know came up to them.

"My name is Sarah. Do you want to jump rope with me?"

"We don't jump rope," Danielle said. "It's too boring."

"I can show you some special jumps and moves I learned from my older sister. She competes in jump rope competitions."

"Okay. We'll try it," Morgan said. "Show us."

Sarah showed Danielle and Morgan some special jumps."This is harder than I thought it would be," Danielle said.

"I guess we won't say that jump roping is boring any more," Morgan said.

Bible Wisdom

You might like to spend time alone, but other activities are just more fun to do with a friend. The Bible tells us:

 **are better than**

—*Ecclesiastes 4:9*

This means that things are better with a friend! A friend can help you with a hard job. Work is more fun when you do it with a friend. Playing is more fun with friends too.

Puzzle Pieces Favorites

Help these girls find a friend with similar interests. Look at what each friend has and then draw a line from the friend on the left to the friend she would play with on the right.

Together Time

Ask each of your friends what her favorite thing to do is. Make time together to do each activity on the list.

Friend #1	Friend #2	Friend #3
_____	_____	_____
_____	_____	_____
_____	_____	_____

Step by Step ✳ The Best Thing About Friends

You've read what friends do for each other — friends listen to each other, friends care when you're sad, friends share and keep secrets, friends like you for who you are, and friends spend time together. But there is one more very special part of friendship. Solve the puzzle below to find out. Look at the word under each line. Write the first letter of the word on the line. When you are done, you'll know the very best thing about friends.

_____   _____ _____ _____ _____ _____ _____

ant   fox   ring   igloo   elephant   neck   dog

_____ _____ _____ _____ _____

lizard   octopus   violin   egg   saw

_____ _____   _____ _____ _____

apple   tree   apron   lamp   lightning

_____ _____ _____ _____ _____.

top   ice   mouse   ear   shell

—*Proverbs 17:17*

What Makes a Good Friend?

Chapter 4

Character traits are words that describe a person, such as "friendly" or "kind".

What character traits do you think a friend should have? Should she be funny? Kind? Fair? There are lots of character traits that make someone a good friend. And you need to have these same traits to be a good friend to others, too!

Kindness

You probably know what it means to be kind. After all, you've heard your parents say, "be kind to your sister" or "be kind to the kitty" since you were small. Being kind to someone means treating him or her in a nice way.

Alexa was going to be late to school! She ran as quickly as she could down the sidewalk and into the

school. She didn't want to go to the office for a tardy slip. She had two already.

Alexa slowed down in the hallway so she wouldn't get into trouble for running.

"The bell hasn't rung yet. I might make it," Alexa thought. She hurried to hang her backpack on her hook in the classroom. It was unzipped and her lunch bag, books, pencils and folders fell out on the floor when she hung it up.

"Oh no," Alexa said. "Now I will be late for sure!"

"No you won't," Rosa said, joining her. "I'll help you."

"Thanks Rosa. That's really nice of you," Alexa said.

Rosa and Alexa quickly picked up the mess and then hurried to their seats. They made it just as the bell rang.

Can you think of a **kind thing** that someone **did for you?**

How did it Make YOU feel?

When people do something kind for you, **it makes you feel good inside.** When you do nice things for others, it helps them feel good, too. What are some acts of kindness that you can do for others?

List **three kind things** you will do for someone else today:

1. _____

2. _____

3. _____

Bible Wisdom

Being kind to others is important. The Bible often mentions kindness. Paul wrote to his friends, *"Therefore as God's chosen people, holy and dearly loved, clothe yourselves with compassion, kindness, humility, gentleness and patience."*

—Colossians 3:12

What Makes a Good Friend?

Connect the dots in the picture to show how one friend is being kind to the other. Color the picture.

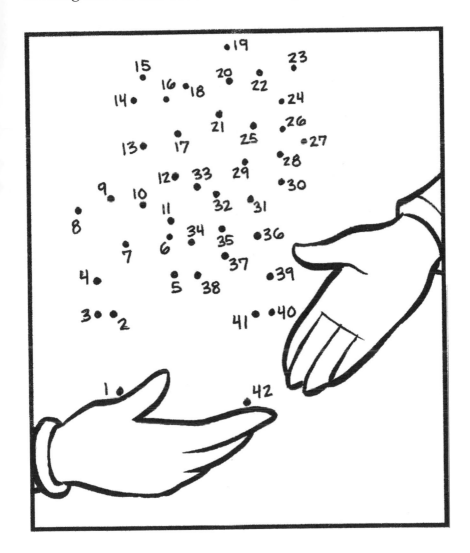

God wants kindness to be part of who we are every day. Just as you put on your clothes in the morning, think of ways you can put on a spirit of kindness.

Loyalty

A loyal friend sticks by you. She's not a person who is friendly one day but then ignores you the next. A loyal friend doesn't say she'll come over to play but then plays with someone else who has better toys. Sometimes our friends change, but a loyal friend is someone you can trust.

●●●●●●●●●●●●●●●●●●●●●●●●●●●●●●●●●●●

Kaitlyn and Sydney were walking home from school and talking about what they were going to do over the weekend.

"Let's ask if you can spend the night Friday night," Kaitlyn said. "We can play games and make popcorn."

"That sounds fun," Sydney said. "Your parents are nice, and so is your brother—even if he is a little goofy."

"Wait up," Cassidy called to the girls. She ran to join them.

"Hi," Sydney greeted Cassidy.

"Can you spend the night Friday night?" Cassidy asked. "My mom said I can have one friend over."

"Kaitlyn and I have already made plans to spend the

night at her house," Sydney said.

"You'd have more fun at my house," Cassidy said. "I have all of the new princess dolls and their accessories. And my dad will take us to the pizza place. We can get lots of tokens and play games together all evening. We'll have lots of fun together."

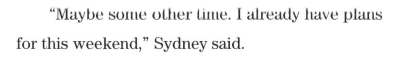

"Maybe some other time. I already have plans for this weekend," Sydney said.

"Your loss! I'll just find someone else who's more fun than you," Cassidy said. She ran to join another group of girls walking home.

Sydney was a loyal friend because she stuck to her plans with Kaitlyn. Cassidy tried to get Sydney to change her mind by telling her she had new toys and that her dad would take them for pizza. But Sydney was a faithful friend because she kept her plans with Kaitlyn.

Bible Wisdom

The Bible talks about loyalty.

Color all the spaces that have a dot in them to find out the Biblical word for loyal.

Proverbs 3:3-4 says, *"Let love and faithfulness never leave you; bind them around your neck, write them on the tablet of your heart. Then you will win favor and a good name in the sight of God and man."*

How loyal are you to your friends? Find out by taking the quiz below. Read the question and then circle the answer that best says what you would do.

 Are You a Loyal Friend?

1. You are jumping rope with your friend, Shimeka, at recess. Then Taylor comes and asks you to play hopscotch with her. What do you do?

A. Go with Taylor

B. Say you'll only go with Taylor if Shimeka can play too

C. Ignore Taylor

2. You are having a birthday party. Your friend Nicole doesn't have much money, but she saves her allowance and buys you a journal and pen. Brittany gives you a deluxe craft kit with all kinds of great stuff. After the party, you hear

Brittany telling Nicole that she's not a very good friend to buy you such a cheap present. What do you do?

A. Wonder if Nicole is such a good friend after all

B. Thank both girls for the presents and tell them that you'll enjoy both of the gifts

C. Pretend you didn't hear Brittany

3. Your teacher tells you to break into groups of two to do a science project. You promise to work with your friend Christina because she needs extra help.

Then Kiara, the class brain, asks you to be her partner. You'd be sure to get an A if you work with Kiara. What do you do?

A. Tell Christina you'll help her find a new partner – you need to work with Kiara and get an A

B. Keep your promise to work with Christina even though you'll have to do more of the work

C. Ask your teacher to give you a partner so you don't have to choose

Which letter did you circle most?

 If you circled mostly A's, then you need to work on becoming a loyal friend. It's okay to be with other friends. But you shouldn't quit an activity with one friend just to do something with someone else. It doesn't matter if she is smarter, faster, or has more cool stuff.

 If you circled mostly B's, you are a faithful friend. You stick with your friend even if they aren't the best on the soccer field or in the classroom. You know that friendship is more important than having cool toys and games.

> **If you circled mostly C's,** you are avoiding making choices. Try to find a way to fix problems such as inviting the other person to play with you. Or you might suggest another activity that everyone likes. If that doesn't work, stick by the friend you agreed to do something with.

Fairness

Has anyone ever told you to be fair? If they have, they were telling you to follow the rules of a game, let someone else have a turn or do what was right. It's not much fun to play with someone who isn't fair.

Haley and Natalie were taking turn shooting baskets to see who could make the most.

"I got that one," Haley said. "I guess I am a better shooter."

Natalie aimed the ball at the basket and was just ready to shoot the ball when Haley pushed her. Natalie's ball missed the basket.

"That wasn't fair," Natalie said. "You pushed me. That wasn't very kind."

"It was an accident," Haley protested. "It's my turn," she said, grabbing the ball.

"No, I get to shoot that one over," Natalie said. "That's only fair. Friends don't treat each other like that."

"You just want more turns! I'm not playing with you anymore," Haley said angrily.

"I'll play with you, Natalie," her friend Tia said. "Haley doesn't play fair. She hurts other people's feelings. I'm not surprised that she doesn't have very many friends."

Have you noticed that people who **don't play fair** often don't have many friends? No one wants to be with someone who cheats or is a bad sport or doesn't take turns. It makes others feel badly inside when friends act that way.

These girls have different opinions about what makes a good friend. What would you say?

Friendliness.
I like a person who is not mean and who cares

**CANDICE
AGE 9**

Loyalty, because I think you should be able to trust a friend.

RACHEL · AGE 9

Nice.
Because if you're not nice someone's feelings could get hurt.

**JORDAN
AGE 7**

Caring,
so you can love each other and nothing can break you apart.

**SHELBIE
AGE 8**

Trust.
Because if you can trust them, you can tell them anything.

**HANNAH
AGE 9**

Playful.
I like a friend to be fun and to play games and sports.

JESSICA · AGE 8

✳ Just for Me! ✳
Bible Wisdom

What does the Bible say will happen if you listen to God's word and seek His wisdom? Use the box code to find out.

Look under the first line. You see 3 ♥. Put your left pointer finger on the 3 and your right pointer finger on the ♥. Bring your fingers together (your left hand moving to the right and your right hand moving down) to where those two symbols meet. You should have your finger on the letter "t". Write "t" on the first line. Continue doing this with each pair of numbers and symbols until you can read the Bible message.

KEY	🐈	🍎	🌸	★	♥
1	a	d	e	f	g
2	h	i	j	l	n
3	o	p	r	s	t
4	u	v	w	y	z

What Makes a Good Friend?

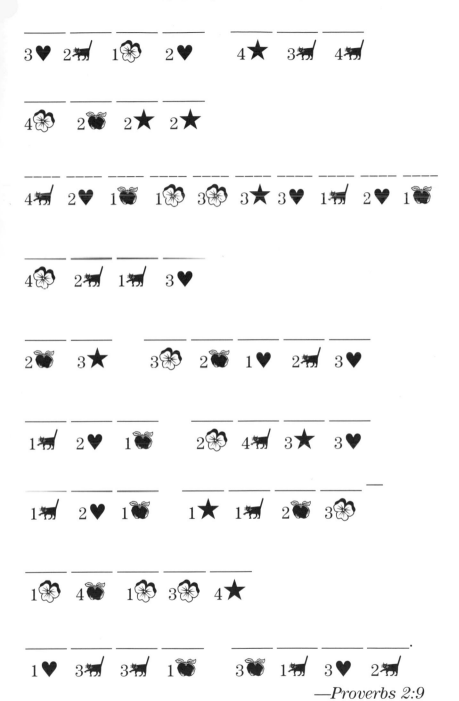

—*Proverbs 2:9*

❂ Friend Chain ❂

You will need at least one friend to do this project with you. The more friends you have working on it, the more fun it will be! And the more friends working together, the longer your chain will be.

You Will Need:

🌼 strips of colored paper

🌼 markers or pencils

🌼 stapler and staples

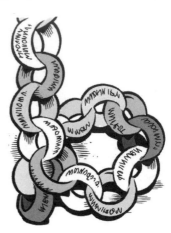

What to do:

🌼 Have the first person choose a color.

🌼 Everyone will use that color paper to write the things they like about that friend (for example, if you choose red, all of your friends will write things that they like about you on the red strips)

🌼 After all the strips are written on, take one strip and staple it to make a circle. Then take a strip of another color and form a circle through the first circle. Staple to form a new circle and continue until all of the strips are in the chain. Hang the chain in your room to remind you of your friends.

Tips on Finding and Making Friends

Chapter 5

Do you want a friend who will play games with you? Would you like a friend to share your secrets? Do you wish you had a friend to play with at recess? Doing things alone is okay, but most activities are more fun with a friend!

What if you don't have friends though?

Maybe you have moved and left your friends behind. Or maybe you attend a new school. Perhaps you are just shy and find it hard to make friends. What should you do?

Read on! This chapter will give you all sorts of ideas about where to meet kids your age and what to do once you meet them.

Step by Step✳ Where to Meet Friends

Think about all the places you might meet friends. Circle the pictures on the following pages that represent places you go or activities that you enjoy.

School playground: look around for other kids who are alone

School lunch room: look for someone who isn't talking to anyone else

Home school field trip: look for someone near your age

Skating rink or swimming pool: look for someone who seems to be having fun

Neighborhood playground: look for someone who isn't with a group

Church: look around your church class or at a special activity for someone who looks friendly

Softball, basketball, soccer or other sports team: look for someone else who enjoys sports

Don't forget, you can also look in your own home for a friend!

Write a letter to God asking Him to help you meet new friends.

Dear God,

_____

_____

_____

Your friend,

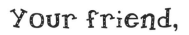

✳Step ᵇʸStep✳ Friendship Starters

Now that you know where to look for friends, it's time to make the first move. Keep in mind, making friends takes time. If you're shy (find it hard to talk to people you don't know), it can take longer. So, be patient and keep praying for God to help you. Here are some friend-making tips to get you started.

Be Friendly

You have to be friendly to make friends. People around you will notice that you're friendly. Start by smiling and saying "hi" when you are around others. Even if you feel shy, you can do that much!

Julia was excited. She was going to be on the Shark's soccer team. She had never been on a team before and thought it would be fun. Julia's mom drove into the parking lot. There were lots of other boys and girls running around. Julia was glad to see that there were so many girls who liked to play soccer. Some were kicking a ball back and forth. Others were in groups talking.

Suddenly Julia felt shy. What if everyone already knew each other? What if she was the only one who didn't know anyone?

Julia tied the laces on her cleats. Then she got out of the car. She had her new pink and silver soccer ball tucked under her  arm. Julia saw another girl who was alone and she had the same color soccer ball! Julia went over to her.

"Hi, I'm Julia. This is my first time playing," she said.

"I'm Jasmine. I played last year. Are you on the Sharks or the Hot Shots team?"

"I'm a Shark."

"Me too! My mom is the coach!" Jasmine said. "Let's practice kicking."

Julia and Jasmine kicked the ball back and forth

until the coach called the team over to start their first practice. Before practice was over, Julia had made friends with Jasmine; they agreed to warm up together before the next practice.

"This is going to be a lot of fun," Julia told her mom on the way home. "Everyone is really friendly. I'm glad I joined the soccer team."

● ●

Julia felt shy at first because she didn't know anyone. Then she met Jasmine and the rest of the Sharks. That made it more fun. Have you ever gone somewhere new and made a friend like Julia did? Write down where and what that was like:

How did you feel before you made friends? What did you do to make some friends?

Puzzle Pieces A-mazing Soccer Friends

Help Julia score the goal! Complete the maze below as Julia's teammate cheers her on.

Bible Wisdom

Being friendly and cheerful will help you make friends more easily. What makes you cheerful? The Bible says, "A happy heart makes the face cheerful."

—*Proverbs 15:13*

Draw a picture below of yourself doing something that makes you happy:

When you're happy inside, your face shows it! Knowing that Jesus loves you can make your heart happy too.

 Get to Know Others

A good way to learn more about someone is to ask them about their family, their hobbies, their pets, or anything else that is unique to them.

Lauren was at the skating rink for Abigail's birthday party. They were both home schooled. Once a month, lots of home school families got together to do fun things. There were so many kids of all ages mixed together that Lauren hadn't gotten to know any of them very well. Abigail's mom invited all of the students near Abigail's age to her party.

Lauren wanted to get to know Abigail better. She skated up next to her.

"Hi! What grade are you in?" she asked.

"I should be in second, but I've worked so far ahead that I'm doing third grade work," Abigail answered. "What grade are you in?"

"I'm in second. Have you always been home schooled?"

"No," Abigail said. "I was in a Christian school in

kindergarten and then my mom decided to home-school me. What about you?"

"I've always been home schooled," Lauren said.

A girl named Marita skated up and started talking to them too. Pretty soon Lauren knew a lot about both

Abigail and Marita. She had fun talking to other home school students during Abigail's party. She couldn't wait to see them

again when all the students got together for a field trip at the end of the month.

● ●

Lauren and Abigail had something in common. They were both home schooled. You will probably find that you have lots of interests and hobbies in common with others around you. **But you won't find out unless you talk with them!**

Bible Wisdom

Asking questions helps you get to know what other people like and are interested in. The Bible tells us that we should think about other people before ourselves. You can read the message for yourself below.

To read the message, just cross out every 'x' and 'z'. Write the rest of the letters in order on the lines below.

Exaczh zof yxzou sxhouxld lzozok xnotz oxnlxy toz xxyouxr zownx zintzerezsts, bxxut zalxso xto tzzhe zinxteresxts xof zotxhers. —*Philippians 2:4*

_____

_____

_____

_____

 Getting to Know Others

How can you find out what other kids like? By asking questions just as Lauren did! Here are some questions you could ask:

What grade are you in?

_____

What is your favorite subject?

_____
_____
_____
_____

Where do you go to school?

_____
_____
_____
_____
_____

How many brothers and sisters do you have? How old are they?

_____
_____
_____
_____

Do you play on any sports teams?

_____
_____
_____

What is your pet's name?

_____
_____

What's your favorite animal?

_____
_____

Do you take any lessons or classes?

_____
_____
_____

Do you go to church? Where is your church?

_____
_____
_____

Do you have any pets? What kind are they?

_____
_____
_____

What does your family like to do together?

_____
_____
_____

✳ Just for Me! ✳

These are only a few of the many questions you could ask. Write some of your own questions below:

Look around for someone that you don't know well and ask him or her some of these questions.

 Ask to Join the Fun

At times you'll find everyone may already be playing or working together at school, at recess or at church. Don't be afraid to ask to join the fun.

Samantha stood watching some girls draw with chalk at recess. She was new to this school. Samantha didn't know many kids yet. She thought about joining the girls who were sitting on the swings talking, but drawing with chalk looked like more fun.

One of the girls looked up and Samantha asked, "May I draw, too?"

"Do you have any chalk?" one of the girls asked.

"No," Samantha answered.

"That's okay, you can share mine," another girl said. "My name's Clara."

"I'm Samantha. Thanks for sharing."

"Let's draw something together," Clara said. "Do you like cats? Let's draw a cat."

Clara was willing to let Samantha draw with her. But sometimes people say "no" when you ask to join the fun.

Has anyone every told you "no" when you wanted to play with them? **How did you feel?**

_____

_____

You might feel sad if you can't join the fun. Other times you might feel mad. If someone doesn't want to play with you, try not to feel hurt. Just look for someone else to play with. **It's even okay to play by yourself sometimes.** You will learn about many activities that are fun to do alone later in this book.

  Bible Wisdom

Clara let Samantha join the fun. When you do good deeds because you love Jesus, you are doing it for Him, too. Jesus says, _"Whatever you did for one of ....these brothers of mine, you did for me."_ —Matthew 25:40.

Jesus told the people that when they gave someone food or clothes, they did it for Him. You can make Jesus happy by asking someone to play with you when she is alone or looks sad.

You said it! Inviting Others

You are playing tag with your friends. You see a girl sitting by herself watching the game. **What would you say to her?** Write your words in the word bubble below.

You are getting ready to sit with all of your friends at lunch when you notice a girl sitting by herself at another table.

What would you say?

_____

_____

You tell a classmate that you are going to a church party on Saturday. She says she doesn't go to church.

What would you say?

_____

_____

Some times you might be the one who asks to join the fun. Other times someone might ask if she can join you. Both of those things are part of being friends.

Look for Things in Common

It's natural to become friends with girls who like the same things as you. That doesn't mean that you enjoy all the same things. But you like at least some of the same activities or favorites. When you're looking for new friends, look for girls who share your hobbies and interests.

Mackenzie had just moved because her dad had a new job. Today her family was going to a picnic where they would meet everyone from her dad's new job. Mackenzie wondered if she'd make any friends.

When Mackenzie's family got to the picnic she looked around for other girls she could play with. She saw a girl near her age doing cartwheels.

"I'm going to go talk to that girl," Mackenzie told her dad.

"Hi," Mackenzie said to the girl. "Are you in gymnastics?"

"Yes, I take lessons every week. My name's Olivia. I haven't seen you at a picnic before."

"I'm new," Mackenzie said. "We just moved here. But I took gymnastics where we lived before. I just learned to do a one-handed cartwheel before we moved."

"Cool. Maybe you can join my gymnastics class," Olivia said.

The girls did cartwheels and front hand springs until it was time to eat. Then Mackenzie took Olivia to meet her family. Mackenzie's mom said she could sign up for Olivia's gymnastics class, too.

Mackenzie found a new friend who shared her interest in gymnastics. When you find someone who likes the same activities as you, you can quickly become friends.

Shared Fun

Below are pictures of activities that you could do with friends. Circle the pictures that show your favorite activities to do.

What are some activities that you like to do with friends that aren't pictured here?

_____

_____

_____

 ## Treat Others the Way You Want to be Treated

Do you like it when a friend shares with you or offers to play your favorite game? Do you enjoy it when a friend asks you to sit with her at lunch or play a special game at recess? Yes? Well, you're not alone! Others like it too! Treating others the way you want to be treated will help you to make friends.

It was raining outside so all the classes were having indoor recess. Most of the second grade students were already playing in groups. Only Michaela, Gabrielle and Amanda weren't playing with anyone.

"Do you want to play together?" Amanda asked Michaela and Gabrielle.

"Sure," Michaela said happily.

"I don't know," Gabrielle said. "Maybe I will just read a book at my desk."

Amanda remembered that Gabrielle didn't have many friends. She was shy and talked in class only if the teacher called on her.

"There are lots of games left on the shelf," Amanda said. "Why don't you choose a game and we'll play it together."

"I'm not very good at games," Gabrielle said. "I'm better at puzzles."

"Okay. You get a puzzle and we'll do it with you," Amanda said.

"That's okay with me, too," Michaela said. "You choose what we do today. Maybe next time you'll want to try a game."

"Thanks," Gabrielle said, going to get a puzzle. They worked together and finished the puzzle just as the bell rang to end recess.

Amanda and Michaela were both willing to do a

puzzle with Gabrielle instead of playing a game. Sometimes treating others the way you want to be treated means letting them have their way or doing things they want to do. But true friends will do the same for you and allow you to have your way sometimes, too!

Bible Wisdom

The verse below from the book of Matthew talks about treating others the way you want to be treated:

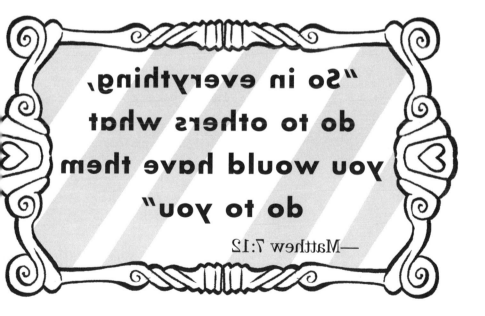

"So in everything, do to others what you would have them do to you."

—Matthew 7:12

What? You can't read it? Oh, that's right. You need to hold it up to a mirror and then you can read it!

God says that people who read his message and don't do it are like those who look in the mirror at their reflection and then walk away forgetting what they look like! That means that God wants us to remember what He says and to do the things He tells us to do in the Bible. One thing He says is to do to treat others the way

you want them to treat you. Sometimes people call this the "Golden Rule" but really it's God's rule. And this rule will help you make new friends.

Make It!

❂ Friends Collage ❂

This is a fun craft to help you think about your friends. You can make this collage with just one friend or with many friends.

▶ You Will Need:

- A large piece of poster board
- Colored paper
- Scissors
- Glue
- Photographs of your friends (like pictures your mom took at your last birthday party or soccer game)

▶ What to do:

- Make a pattern of a triangle, circle, rectangle or square onto heavy paper.
- Place the pattern you just made onto your colored paper and trace it, then cut it out.

※ Do this until you have a frame for each picture you want to use (you don't have to have a frame for every picture)

※ Put a small line of glue around the edge of a picture, then put the paper frame on top and press down to glue frame to photo and let it dry

※ Do this until all your pictures have frames

※ Decide how you are going to arrange the photographs on the page (you can experiment with the photographs going different directions and overlapping)

※ Glue the framed photos to the poster board

※ Write captions (funny sayings about each picture) or title the collage any way you like

※ Let it dry, then hang the collage in your room

Having lots of friends is fun.

But do you have one special friend —
A best friend?

Best Friends

Chapter 6

Having friends is good. Having a best friend is great! Think of all the things you can share with a best friend. You can share your thoughts, your dreams, your fun times, your sad times and so much more!

Your best friend enjoys many of the same activities as you. You might both like reading or in-line skating. You might be in dance or gymnastics lessons together. Usually your best friend is the friend you spend the most time with.

 **S**helby was riding her scooter at the park with her friends Kaylee, Laura, Ginny and Abby. After going around the path twice, they sat on the swings talking about school and their plans for the weekend.

"I have to go now," Abby said looking at the time on her watch.

"Me too," Kaylee and Laura said. They got on their scooters and headed for home.

Shelby turned to Ginny. "Maybe you can sleep over at my house tonight. We can make a picture collage for each other."

"Okay. Can you have your mom call my mom?" Ginny asked. "If your mom calls, my mom will say yes."

Shelby's mom called Ginny's mom and made plans for Ginny to spend the night.

"I like Abby, Kaylee and Laura. But you're my best friend" Ginny said. "We always do fun things together."

Shelby has lots of friends she likes to be with: Abby, Kaylee, Laura and Ginny. They ride scooters, talk to each other on the phone and play at recess. But the friend Shelby likes to be with the most is Ginny. That's because she and Ginny have things they like to do just with each other like play games and make crafts.

They are best friends.

Best Buddies

Do you have a best friend? If you do, try this fun quiz to see how much you and your best friend know about each other. Both of you need a piece of paper and a pencil.

There are ten sentences on the next page. Read the sentences aloud. First, write down the answer that fits your friend. Then write down the answer that fits you. Your friend should do the same.

For example, the sentence might say: My friend's favorite color is _____.

Write down the color that you think your friend likes the best. Then in a separate column write down the color that you like the best. Your friend will write the color she thinks that you like the best and then the color she likes the best. Your paper might look like this:

Ginny	Me
1. Red	Blue

Sometimes you might have the same answer twice because you like the same things. Do this for each question.

My Friend

Me

1. If my friend could have any pet, she'd want a

_____.

1. If I could have any pet, I'd want a

_____.

2. The food my friend loves the most is

_____.

2. The food I love the most is

_____.

3. My friend's favorite holiday is

_____.

3. My favorite holiday is

_____.

4. My friend's favorite sport is

_____.

4. My favorite sport is

_____.

5. The book my friend likes the most is

_____.

5. The book I like the most is

_____.

6. The school subject my friend likes the most is

_____.

6. The school subject I like the most is

_____.

7. The thing my friend likes to do most at recess is

_____.

7. The thing I like to do most at recess is

_____.

8. My friend's favorite music group is

_____.

8. My favorite music group is

_____.

9. The movie my friend has watched the most is

_____.

9. The movie I have watched the most is

_____.

10. Last year my friend went on vacation to _____.

10. Last year I went on vacation to

_____.

Now, read your answers to each other and see how many you got right. If you got most of them right, you know a lot about your best friend. If you didn't, then you will have fun finding out more about your best friend. You can make up your own questions and try again!

Bible Wisdom

God has a special command for us. To find out what it is, use the speedometer to help you. Each speed has a letter assigned to it. Look at the speed under each line and write the letter that matches that speed.

____ ____   ____ ____ ____ ____   ____ ____ ____
40   80   10   50   40   40   5   45   15

____ ____   ____ ____ ____ ____:
30   60   65   25   30   60

____ ____ ____ ____   ____ ____ ____ ____
35   50   75   20   20   5   10   25

____ ____ ____ ____ ____   ____ ____   ____
50   65   25   20   55   5   60   30

____ ____ ____ ____   ____ ____ ____ ____ ____
25   5   75   20   35   50   75   20   15

____ ____ ____.
80   50   70   —John 15:12

Make It!

❂ Stand Up Photo

Best friends love each other. Below is a craft that you can make for your best friend or you can both make one together. You will need an adult's help for this one!

You can make a cool stand-up photo of yourself and a best friend.

You Will Need:

❊ A photograph of you and a friend (one copy for each person doing the craft – you might want to have it made larger so the figures in the photo are larger. Try to use a photo where you and your friend are close together

❊ Glue

❊ Foam board (available in craft stores.) Make sure to get a piece that is as big as the picture you are using for this craft.

❋ Scissors or craft knife

❋ Two strips of wood for the base - they need to be
as long as the picture they will hold

▶ What to do:

❋ Cut around the outline of the picture, making
sure to keep you and your friend attached (don't
cut yourselves apart unless you want to make
separate pictures of each)

❋ Spread glue evenly over the entire back of
the picture

❋ Glue the picture to the foam board and let dry

❋ Have a parent help you to carefully cut the foam
board around the picture using scissors or a craft
knife and leave the bottom edge flat

❋ Apply glue to one side of each board and place
the bottom of the picture between the boards

❋ Test that the boards form a base that will hold
the picture upright

❋ Let it dry, then set it up so you can see it

Bible Buddies

This story is about two friends. Even though they are boys, you can still learn a lot about friendship from the story.

The Bible tells us about two special friends, David and Jonathan. Do you remember who David was? He was the shepherd boy who killed the giant Goliath with a sling and a stone. After that, David became very important to King Saul and David was given a high rank in the army.

The people of Israel loved David and he became very popular. One day when he got back from battle

the people sang, "Saul has slain his thousands, and David his tens of thousands." That made King Saul mad. They were saying that David was

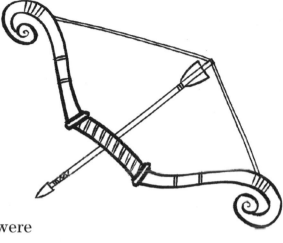

more successful than King Saul. From then on, King Saul was jealous and tried to hurt David.

Jonathan was King Saul's son. Jonathan should have been king after Saul, but God chose David to be the next king instead. Jonathan didn't mind that David would be king instead of him. He and David were best friends. Jonathan was sad that his father wanted to harm David.

David was invited to a feast with King Saul. He didn't know if the king planned to harm him at the feast or not. He decided not to go. He asked Jonathan to find out if King Saul planned to harm him. They made a plan. David would hide outside. Jonathan would find out whether or not his father was going to harm David. Jonathan would then go outside and shoot three arrows.

Then he would send a boy to find get the arrows. Jonathan told David, "If I say, 'Look, the arrows are on this side of you; bring them here' then you are safe. But if I say, 'Look, the arrows are beyond you,' then you must go because you are in danger."

When it was time for the feast to begin, Saul saw that David was missing. He was angry. He told Jonathan, "As long as David is alive, you won't be king. Bring him to me because he must die."

Jonathan was very sad. He shot the arrows the way he had planned. Then he said, "Isn't the arrow beyond you? Hurry! Go quickly!" David knew he must leave quickly and find a safe place to stay.

Jonathan went quickly to David to say goodbye.

Bible Wisdom

Jonathan told David, *"Go in peace, for we have sworn friendship with each other in the name of the Lord."* —1 Samuel 20:42

Best Friends

Do you have a best friend who loves you the way Jonathan loved David? Draw a picture of your best friend:

Write a prayer to God and ask him to help you be a friend to your best friend like Jonathan was to David.

Dear God,

_____

_____

_____

Amen

❋Step by Step❋ No Best Friend Yet?

No best friend yet? **No problem!** Be the best friend to others that you can be. Remember the list of traits to look for in a friend: kindness, loyalty, fairness, honesty, giving, and caring. Ask God to help you have all of these traits and to bring you a special best friend.

A Friendly Maze

Help the boy collect the three arrows that Jonathan shot to warn David.

101

⊙ Friendship Crackers

Jonathan gave David special gifts because they were good friends. Jonathan gave David his own robe and tunic, as well as his sword, bow and belt. Your parents probably wouldn't like it if you gave your clothes away and you probably don't have a sword or bow, but you can make the awesome craft below for a friend.

 ## You Will Need:

 Empty toilet paper rolls

 Wrapping paper or tissue paper to cover the toilet paper roll

 Tape

 Scissors

 Two pieces of curling ribbon (curl tie) about 18 inches long

 Wrapped candy

 Very small toys, stickers or other small treats

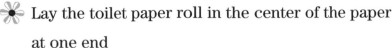

What to do:

❋ Lay the toilet paper roll in the center of the paper at one end

❋ Tape the wrapping or tissue paper to the roll

❋ Roll the toilet paper roll to the other end so that all the wrapping paper is wrapped securely around the toilet paper roll and tape it

❋ There should be extra paper off each end of the toilet paper roll

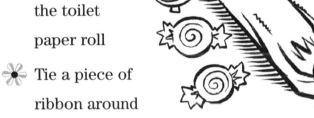

❋ Tie a piece of ribbon around the extra paper on one end so that it is closed

❋ Fill the roll with candy or other small items

❋ Tie the other end closed with ribbon

❋ Have a parent help you curl the ribbon using scissors

❋ Give it to your friend

When Things Go Wrong

Chapter 7

You probably have a lot of fun with your friends. You play games, talk, laugh, eat lunch together, talk on the phone and maybe even sleep over at each

other's houses. Those are good times that you will remember for a long time.

 Once in a while though, friends have problems. They hurt each other's feelings, say unkind things and maybe even say that they don't want to be friends anymore. Has that ever happened to you? If so, you need a life preserver to help rescue your friendship!

Ashley and Claire were playing a board game at school. "I just need to roll a six, and I win again," bragged Ashley.

"You keep cheating," Claire said. "Once you said you rolled a four, and it was a five. And then the next turn you moved six spaces, but you only counted to five. That's why you keep winning. It's not important who wins. A game should be fun. But it's not fun when you cheat."

"I do not cheat! You just don't pay attention. You're not very good at games," Ashley said.

"If that's how you feel, then I'm not playing with you anymore!" Claire said.

Claire went to find another friend to play with while Ashley picked up the game pieces and put the game away.

Sometimes your friendships will be smooth sailing. But occasionally, you might run into a friendship iceberg! These icebergs threaten to sink your friendship. Here are some common ones to watch out for. But don't despair! For each iceberg there's a life preserver to keep the friendship afloat!

Bossiness Iceberg

There will be problems when one friend always wants to be in charge. No one wants to be bossed around all the time.

Friendship Life Preserver

Take turns choosing what to do. One recess time you choose what to play on the playground, and the next time someone else chooses.

Can you think of a time when you were bossy?

 What happened?

_____

_____

Bible Wisdom

Arrange these words on the seashells on the next page to read God's solution to bossiness. Some have been filled in to help you.

Fill in: **not but of   the to only own to**

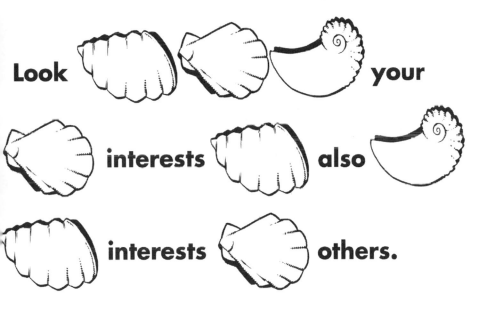

Look _____ _____ _____ your

_____ interests _____ also _____

_____ interests _____ others.

—Philippians 2:4

 ## Jealousy Iceberg

When a friend wants what another friend has, it will cause problems. You can be jealous about the way someone looks, the things that they are good at, or the things they own.

Friendship Life Preserver

Be thankful for the things you have and

109

don't think about the things you wished you had instead.

Can you think of a time when you wanted what your friend had?

Bible Wisdom

The Bible says, *"Let the peace of Christ rule in your hearts.... And be thankful."*

—Colossians 3:15

How Thankful are You?

Take the quiz below to find out.

Read each sentence and circle the letter that sounds the most like you.

1. Your dad brings home a present for both you and your brother. Your brother's is larger. You:

A. Think it's not fair that your brother's present is larger

B. Think it doesn't matter as long as your present is something cool

C. Are happy to get a present for no reason

2. You plan to have
your birthday party at the
skating rink. Then the
family car breaks down
and costs your parents a
lot of money to fix it. Now
you have to have a cake
and games at your house.
You:

A. Think you should get your skating party anyway

B. Hope your friends won't mind the change in plans

C. Are happy just to be celebrating your birthday
   no matter where your party is

3. You are going to get a new bike. You want one
with different speeds and hand brakes, but your dad
says you're not ready for that kind. You:

A. Think your dad is treating you like a baby

B. Hope he'll get you the kind you want next year

C. Are glad to be getting a new bike

Which letter did you circle the most?

If you circled mostly A's: You are having trouble being thankful for the things you get. You want something better or something more. Ask God to help you have a more thankful heart.

If you circled mostly B's: You are usually thankful but you'd still rather have something better than what you have. Accept what you are given and don't forget to say "thanks."

If you circled mostly C's: You are thankful for what you get even if it's not exactly what you want. You know that sometimes you can't have the more expensive things and are happy that you got what you did. Good for you! Thankfulness makes God happy.

Bragging Iceberg: No one likes to hear someone else brag. It's definitely a way to make others feel sad — and mad! When you talk about how good you are at something or how much you have, you are telling others that you think you are better than they are.

Friendship Life Preserver:

Make sure that you always play fairly. If you win more than others do, encourage them. If you make better grades, find ways to help them do better. Let other people praise your work. Don't praise your own work too much!

Bible Wisdom

Hold up this message to a mirror to read what the Bible says about bragging:

"Let another praise you,
and not your own mouth;
someone else and
not your own lips."
—Proverbs 27:2

Teasing Iceberg: Have you ever been teased for being taller or

shorter than others? How about for having freckles or wearing glasses? For being slower than others or missing the ball in a game? If you have, you know that teasing hurts. And teasing can ruin a friendship.

Friendship Life Preserver: Accept your friends the way they are. Encourage them when they are slow, miss a ball, don't understand a math problem or look different than other girls. Friends should build each other up, not tear each other down.

Do you have a friend who gets teased? What can you say to her?

_____

_____

Bible Wisdom

The Bible says, *"A word aptly spoken is like apples of gold in settings of silver."* —Proverbs 25:11

Step by Step Fixing a Fight

Even if you practice all of the ideas in this chapter you might still find yourself out of sorts with a friend. Here are some ideas for fixing the problem.

✳ **Talk to your friend calmly and kindly.** Yelling and name-calling will only make things worse. God says, *"A gentle answer turns away wrath, but a harsh word stirs up anger."* —Proverbs 15:1

✳ **Talk about the problem.** Say what you think the problem is. Then let your friend say what she thinks the problem is. Be sure to listen. God says, *"Everyone should be quick to listen, slow to speak and slow to become angry."* —James 1:19

✳ **Find a way to solve the problem.** You might need to give in or maybe you both need to give in a little to find a solution that works for both of you. God says, *"Seek peace and pursue it."* —Psalm 34:14

✳ **Be sure to say, "I'm sorry" when you are wrong.** Be sure to say, "I forgive you" when your friend is wrong. God says, *"Be kind and compassionate to one another, forgiving each other, just as in Christ God forgave you."* —Ephesians 4:32

Fixing the Problem

Do you remember the story at the beginning of this chapter about Ashley and Claire? They ended up quitting the game and being mad at each other. Let's see if we can fix the story and help them handle the problem in a better way.

Ashley and Claire were playing a board game at school. "I just need to roll a six, and I win again," bragged Ashley.

"You keep cheating," Claire said. "Once you said you rolled a four, and it was a five. And then the next turn you moved six spaces, but you only counted to

five. That's why you keep winning. It's not important who wins. A game should be fun but it's not fun when you cheat."

"I do not cheat! You just don't pay attention. You're not very good at games," Ashley said.

"If that's how you feel, then I'm not playing with you anymore!" Claire said.

Claire went to find another friend to play with while Ashley picked up the game pieces and put the game away.

This is getting bad. Let's help them out!

Write your name on the lines below.

Just then _____ walked up. "What's wrong?" _____ asked.

"She's cheating! She never moves the right amount of spaces," Claire said angrily. "And she said I'm not good at games."

"I did not cheat," Ashley said.

"Do you think that you might have counted wrong by accident?" _____ asked.

"Maybe," Ashley admitted.

"Sometimes I do have problems with games. But I don't cheat on purpose!"

"I'm sorry that I said you were

cheating," Claire said. "I can help you when you need it."

"I don't like to say I need help," Ashley said. "My mom says sometimes I have a problem with pride. I'm sorry I said you weren't good at games. Do you want to play again?"

"Sure," Claire said. "And _____ _____ can play with us too."

•••••••••••••••••••••••••••••••••••

Good job! It looks like another friendship is rescued! You can do the same thing when you have problems with your friends. Talk about the problem in a calm, kind way and look for a solution that is fair to everyone.

Fun Together, Fun Alone

We've talked all about all kinds of friends in this book. This chapter will give you several games, crafts and activities to do together with friends. You can do them with brothers or sisters, too. There are also some that you can do alone as well as with a friend. Some of the crafts and activities require supplies and others don't. There will be a list of what you need at the beginning of each activity. **Have fun doing these activities** with a group of friends, a best friend, a special friend or by yourself!

Step by Step Games to Play with Friends

✪ Balloon Game

 You Will Need

 Two or more players

 Balloons

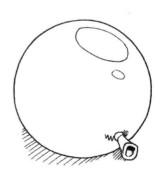

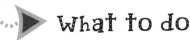

What to do

* The first player throws her balloon into the air and must hit it with one hand to keep it in the air while everyone else counts the number of times the player hits it before the balloon hits the ground

* Stop at 50 hits if you get that far; if the balloon pops, you're out

* The next player does the same thing. If she hits it more times than the first player, the first player must sit down. If not, the second player sits down. If both have 50 hits, both stay standing

* Do this again and the person with the highest number of hits keeps standing

* Continue until only one person is standing — that person is the winner

❂ Bible Character Guess

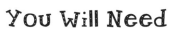

You Will Need

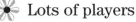

* Lots of players

▶ What to do

❋ Player one thinks of a famous Bible character

❋ The player stands up and acts out that Bible character with no words or sound effects

❋ The first person to guess the character's name acts out another character

⊙ Chain

▶ You Will Need

❋ Lots of players

▶ What to do

❋ One person is "it"

❋ The other players run around the yard

❋ When "it" tags a player, that player and "it" grab hands or wrists

❋ Both players can then tag other players and everyone tagged joins hands or wrists to make one long chain

* The last person tagged becomes "it" for the next game

❂ In The Middle

▶ You Will Need

* Three or more players
* A ball

▶ What to do

* Two players stand on the opposite sides of the yard from each other
* The other player or players stand between those players
* The two players throw the ball to each other without letting the players in the middle catch the ball

125

If one of the players in the middle catches the ball, the person who threw the ball goes in the middle and the person who caught the ball becomes a thrower

⊙ Potato in the Pot

 ### ▶ You Will Need

- Two or more players
- Small ball or bean bag
- Laundry basket

▶ What to do

- Stand in a line side by side in front of the basket
- Take turns throwing the ball or bag into the basket
- If you make it, take a step back. If you miss, sit down. You're out!
- Keep doing this until everyone is out. The player who can throw the ball from the farthest away wins

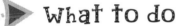# ❀ Tight Squeeze

▶ You Will Need

 Lots of friends or family members

▶ What to do

 Pick one person to be "it"

 "It" hides while everyone else counts to 50. "It" is careful to pick a hiding place that is big enough for everyone to join her

 Search for the hidden player

 When you find the player, hide in with her but don't tell anyone else where she is

 Once everyone has found the hidden player, the game is over

 The first person who found the hidden player is "it" the next time

127

Step by Step ✳ Activities You Can Do Alone or with a Friend

Make It!

❂ Animal Diorama

 ## You Will Need

 Shoebox

 Pictures of animals or scenery cut from magazines or greeting cards

 Crayons or markers

 Small plastic animals

 ## What to do

Sit the shoebox on its side

Glue animal or scenery pictures to the back of the shoebox for background scenery

 Use crayons or markers to color in grass, lakes or anything else

 Sit the animals in the foreground

 Do the same thing using home, school, the zoo, pets or other themes

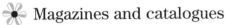

❂ Book of Favorites

▶ You Will Need

- ❋ Magazines and catalogues
- ❋ Scissors
- ❋ Glue
- ❋ Construction paper
- ❋ Yarn
- ❋ Hole punch

▶ What to do

- ❋ Label each piece of construction paper with a category such as "food," "fun times," "animals" and so on
- ❋ Cut out pictures to go on the pages (you might cut out pictures of pizza, spaghetti and pudding to go on the food page – you can do this for as many categories as you want)
- ❋ Compare your favorites to your friend's favorites and see if you have some of the same favorites!

⊙ Cat Shaped Snack

▶ You Will Need

- ✳ Three slices of bread
- ✳ Favorite sandwich filling
- ✳ Knife (with adult help)
- ✳ Grapes
- ✳ Piece of uncooked spaghetti
- ✳ Raisins

▶ What to do

- ✳ Make a whole sandwich and a half sandwich
- ✳ Cut a large circle out of the whole sandwich
- ✳ Cut off the points of the half sandwich to make ears
- ✳ Use grapes for the eyes and nose
- ✳ Line up raisins for the mouth
- ✳ Break the spaghetti into pieces and use for whiskers
- ✳ Experiment with other foods and make your own animal face

❁ Fingerprint Fun

▶ You Will Need

- Paper
- Washable ink pad
- Pencils or markers

▶ What to do

- Make fingerprints on a piece of paper
- Use the pencil or markers to add arms, legs, eyes and whatever else to make your own creatures

☼ Greeting Card Books

 You Will Need

❊ Four or five new or used greeting cards

❊ Yarn

❊ Hole punch

 What to do

❊ Carefully remove the backs of each card so you have only the picture

❊ Punch holes along the side of each card three inches apart

❊ Lace the yarn through the holes to hold the cards together and make a book

❊ Give the book to an older friend or mail to a far-away friend

❁ Melted Crayon Craft

▶ You Will Need

- ❋ Old crayons
- ❋ Knife or peeler (with adult help)
- ❋ Wax paper
- ❋ Iron (with adult help)
- ❋ Paper towel

▶ What to do

- ❋ Have a parent help you use the knife or peeler to make crayon shaving of different colors
- ❋ Drop shavings of different colors on a piece of wax paper (5"x7" or 8"x10" or any size)
- ❋ Cover with a piece of wax paper of the same size
- ❋ Cover the wax paper with a paper towel
- ❋ Have a parent press the hot iron against the paper towel long enough to melt the crayon shavings
- ❋ Try different color combinations and arrangements

✿ Mouse in a Cage

 **You Will Need**

❋ Peeled banana

❋ Lemon juice

❋ Pastry brush

❋ Knife

❋ Almond slices

❋ Raisins

❋ Soft cream cheese

❋ Orange

❋ Toothpicks

❋ Uncooked spaghetti

❋ Whole almonds or peanuts

 What to do

❋ With adult help, cut 1½ inch piece of banana

❋ Brush with a little lemon juice and let dry

❋ Attach two almond slices for ears using soft cream cheese to help them stick

* Using soft cream cheese, attach two raisins for eyes

* Using soft cream cheese, attach a whole peanut or almond for nose

* Break a piece of spaghetti into six small pieces and arrange around nose for whiskers

* Slice an unpeeled orange into slices ½ inch thick

* Using a slice from the middle, lay it flat on the table and poke toothpicks into the peel around the edge for cage bars.

* Attach another slice to the top to complete the cage

Make It!

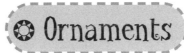

⊙ **Ornaments**

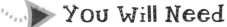

▶ **You Will Need**

* Crayola™ model magic

* Cookie cutters in fun shapes

* Phillips head screw driver

* Rolling pin

* Ribbon or yarn

135

▶ What to do

❋ Roll the model magic to about ½ inch thick

❋ Use the cookie cutters to make shapes

❋ Punch a hole in the top with the screwdriver

❋ Let it dry

❋ Tie a piece of ribbon through the hole to hang the ornaments

❋ Make some for your friends and family as well as for yourself

⚙ Paint Blobs

▶ You Will Need

❋ Paint shirt

❋ Heavy paper

❋ Finger or poster board paint

❋ Crayons

▶ What to do

❋ Fold a sheet of paper in two, crease, then unfold it

❋ Drop a few drops of paint on one side of the paper

❋ Refold the paper so the paint smears

❋ Unfold the paper, look at all the patterns and try to find shapes and "pictures"

❋ Use crayons to turn the blobs into a picture

Other things you might want to do

when you are alone are:

* Read the Psalms

* Re-read a favorite book

* Try a book by an author whose books you've never read before.

* Start a journal. Each day or week, write about something different. One time you might write a little bit about each of your friends. The next time you could write about your teachers. Write about your favorite books or authors or your favorite TV shows. Try to think of something new to write about each time you write. You might write every day or twice a week or even once a month

* Make a scrapbook of all your friends. Have one page for each friend. On that page, put pictures of your friend and write about her

※ Do a puzzle

※ Do a craft project. You can get easy craft kits at a discount store or craft store. Try something new like sand art or string art

※ Clean your room. Fill a box for the homeless shelter with toys and games you don't use anymore

Have fun doing these activities!

You can think up other activities to do with your friends or on your own. Write some of your ideas here:

_____

_____

_____

So, after all this talk about friends, who is the

Best Friend of all?

Jesus: The Best Friend of All

Chapter 9

Having a lot of friends is great! So is having a best friend. Having special friends who are different from you is good, too. But having Jesus as your very best friend is the most awesome of all!

Savannah lay awake. She was at church camp for the first time, and she couldn't sleep. It was dark here, and the bed wasn't nearly as comfortable as her bed at home. The mattress was lumpy and it smelled funny. She could hear strange sounds outside. Savannah's counselor said the sounds were just cricket and frog sounds, but Savannah wasn't sure. She wished her mom was here with her.

Savannah knew that Jesus was with her. Jesus was the friend who went everywhere with her and always listened. "I'm not sure I like it here, Jesus," Savannah whispered. "I don't know most of the other kids and there are strange sounds outside. Help me sleep and help me make friends."

Savannah decided to try and say all the verses she knew by memory to herself. The verses would help her remember that Jesus cared about her no matter where she was.

• •

Do you remember the things that friends do for each other? (They are listed in chapters 2 and 3). Did you know that Jesus always does those things for you? That's because He's the best friend of all. Here's how He does each one.

Friends listen to each other. Jesus hears you when you pray. The Bible says, *"You will pray to Him, and He will hear you"* (Job 22:27). This was true for Job back when it was written, and it's true for you today. Jesus wants to hear about your happy times and your sad times. He wants you to tell Him about your problems and your accomplishments. Is there something that you want to tell Jesus about today? Write it in the word bubble below.

Friends care when you're sad. Jesus wants to fill your heart with joy. The Bible tells us how God replaces sorrow with joy. Psalm 126:3 says, *"The Lord has done great things for us, and we are filled with joy."* When you are feeling sad you can talk to Jesus about it. Remember all the good things He has done for you, and ask Him to fill your heart with joy.

Can you think of some **good things** that Jesus has done for you? List them below.

_____

_____

_____

Think about these things when you feel sad.

Friends keep secrets. There isn't a verse in the Bible that says that Jesus keeps secrets. In fact, He tells His Father, God, everything! But that's okay. It's a good thing to have God in on your secrets. And, He already knows the secrets of your heart before you even tell Him. 1 Chronicles 28:9 tells us that *"the Lord searches every heart and understands every motive."* That means that God not only knows everything that you've ever done, but why you did it! You can share all your secrets with Jesus.

Friends like you for who you are. Jesus loves you just the way you are. God created you in a very special way. He has a plan just for you. Because of Jesus' death, you are accepted into God's family just the way you are. Romans 15:7 says, *"Accept one another, then, just as Christ accepted you."*

Jesus will never tell you that you are too fat or too skinny, too tall or too short. He'll never tell you that you need to run faster or jump rope better. Jesus loves you just the way you are.

Friends spend time together. Jesus not only spends time with you; He's with you all the time. His promise to you is, *"Never will I leave you; never will I forsake you."* —Hebrews 13:5

Put a check mark by all the times that Jesus is with you.

☐ at school

☐ at the park

☐ during a soccer game

☐ during the night

☐ when you're sick

☐ when you're sad

☐ at church

☐ in the car

Did you put a check mark by all of them? You should have because Jesus is the friend who is always with you!

Friends love at all times. Jesus not only loves you, He loves you so much that He died for your sins so that you can be with Him in heaven. John 15:12-13 says, *"My command is this: Love each other as I have loved you. Greater love has no one than this, that he lay down his life for his friends."*

This is how much Jesus loves you:

✳ Jesus was living with His father, God, in a wonderful place called heaven. God wanted everyone to be with Them in heaven.

✳ People did wrong things and because of that, no one could go to heaven and live with God.

✳ God had another plan. Jesus would live on earth but would never sin.

145

✳ Just for Me! ✳

In Bible times, people offered sacrifices for sin. That means that they killed special animals to show that they were sorry for their sins. Jesus was the sacrifice for us when He died on the cross to pay the price for our sins so that we can live with Him in heaven forever.

✳ Jesus didn't stay dead. He rose again the third day. He defeated death.

✳ Jesus wants you to believe that He died for you. He wants to be your best friend!

> # Isn't that great news?

Can you write a special prayer to Jesus thanking Him for loving you enough to die for you so you can be with Him forever in heaven?

Dear Jesus,

_____

_____

_____

Thank you for loving me! I love you, too!

Make It!

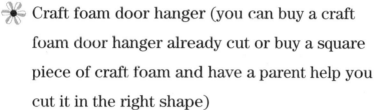

✿ Friend Door Hanger

Of all the friends you'll ever have, Jesus is the best of all. Here's a craft to remind you that you're a friend of Jesus.

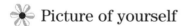

You Will Need:

- Craft foam door hanger (you can buy a craft foam door hanger already cut or buy a square piece of craft foam and have a parent help you cut it in the right shape)

- Picture of yourself

- Foam shapes (you can buy them precut or buy squares of foam and cut your own shapes or you can decorate with markers)

- Markers or stick-on foam letters

What to do:

❋ Letter the words "Friend of Jesus" or use stick on letters to make the words

❋ Cut your picture into a shape that will fit on the foam door hanger (you may want to turn a drinking glass upside down over the picture and trace around it to make your picture the right size)

❋ Glue your picture to the door hanger

❋ Decorate with foam shapes or markers

A different way to do it:

Use a cross shape and glue three or four small magnets on the back to stick it to your refrigerator

These are great reminders that
Jesus is your Best Friend Forever!

Answers

Page 21: Bible Wisdom Word Scrabble

Pleasant words are... sweet to the soul. —Proverbs 16:24

Page 27: Train Car Verse

A trustworthy man keeps a secret. —Proverbs 11:13

Page 36: Bible Wisdom Word Puzzle

Accept one another... just as Christ accepted you.
—Romans 15:7

Page 41: The Best Thing About Friends

A friend loves at all times. —Proverbs 17:17

Page 47: Kindness Connect-the-Dots

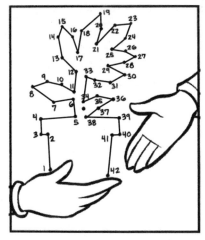

Page 50: Bible Wisdom Fill-In

Picture reveals the word "Faithful"

Page 57: Bible Wisdom Secret Message

Then you will understand what is right and just and fair— every good path. —Proverbs 2:9

Page 67: A-Mazing Soccer Friends

Page 71: Bible Wisdom Hidden Code

Each of you should look not only to your own interests, but also to the interests of others. —Philippians 2:4

Page 83: Bible Wisdom Mirror Message

So in everything, do to others what you would have them do to you. —Matthew 7:12

✳ Just for Me! ✳

Page 93: Speedometer Verse

My command is this: love each other as I have loved you.
—John 15:12

Page 101: A Friendly Maze

Page 109: Bible Wisdom Seashell Puzzle

Look not only to your own interests but also to the interests of others. —Philippians 2:4

Page 113: Bible Wisdom Mirror Message

Let another praise you, and not your own mouth; someone else and not your own lips. —Proverbs 27:2